Flow of Thought

A Collection of Poetry

By Robyn Romanoff

Edited by

Shay Siegel *and* Michael Dotsikas

ISBN 978-0-9961450-4-6

First Edition

10 9 8 7 6 5 4 3 2 1

Porch Time Publishing, LLC

New York

www.porchtimepublishing.com

(Printed in the U.S.)

Dedication

This book is for all the people who influenced these words regardless of the type of vibration you sent through me. I also would like to dedicate this book to myself; the completion of this project was an important goal.

But most importantly, I would like to dedicate this book to you, the reader. I hope to genuinely connect with you, and perhaps help you find connection to yourself. Thank you for taking the time to read.

Table of Contents

Life

Why I Write

A Haiku

I write to find truth

That only comes forth written,

Otherwise stays lost.

I am Made of Seaglass

Molded in an image,
it had a purpose,
it had a place.
Fashioned to be used,
But then came the crash.
It shattered all around,
lying in pieces,
broken.
Then thrown away.
Enduring more,
smash after smash.
Beaten down,
pummeled around,
until one day, it ended.
Emerged in new form,
no longer jagged,
not broken.
Beautifully and uniquely shaped,
perfectly imperfect.

Sunset

I had a dream about a sunset.

Awed by the vibrant colors, the muted hues.

The cotton candy skies, the pale set of blues.

the way it glowed so intensely.

In that dream about a sunset,

I do not know if someone was next to me.

I do not know if I was where I was supposed to be.

Overtaken by limitless sky, so open and free.

Oh, how it always takes my breath away.

I had a dream about a sunset.

I wish it was where I could stay.

Happy Thought

It dances

from the crown of my head

to the bottoms of my feet,

soothing my core, my soul,

elevating mood,

creating an aura

that shines bright.

It leaves behind

a soft smile

upon my face,

one that people see

as they pass by.

They smile back.

A moment

of delight

is created.

All from

one

happy

thought.

Solo Beach Walk

The rocky beaches of the north shore
place the smile on my face today.

As I walk over each unique stone,

I am in awe of the quietude of this place.

I am at peace as I watch the gentle wave

come up to kiss the shoreline.

Sharing the view with the surrounding birds,

together we appreciate the ambiance of nature.

Along my walk I ponder all-encompassing life questions.

Mostly I query the value of another.

But then I spot a piece of seaglass and smile with the sun,

knowing in time, there will be the one.

I take home with me the small treasures of the day

along with a feeling of tranquility.

With a humbled perspective,

I feel grateful for my time on the beach

in the solitude of my own company.

The Whole Picture

The stroke of a brush
leaves behind a mark.
At times, it is willed with intent,
others it is drawn from emotion.
Each mark holds energy
when viewed up closely.
They become troubling
to decipher on their own.
An onlooker may get lost
in part of an image.
Until a step back is taken
in efforts to see
the intricate web of story
behind every painted element.
Until that time comes,
one may never understand
the deep complexity of
the whole picture.

Self-Honesty is Hard

The back and forth is unyielding
with life in different perspectives.
Each choice I make I question.
Pressured by my own decisions
I strive to live in the moment,
but at times I wander away.
Lost in the preplan of the future
has me crazed on my day to day.
I do not know what I truly want,
or if candor is something I possess.
Years of challenge have taken a toll.
Not knowing which version of me is best,
the fatigue has set, and I am out of breath.
The answer is far out of sight.
Honestly, self-honesty is hard.
Truth is only unveiled when I write.

I Want to Feel

I want to feel alive, empowered by vibrations around me.

I want to feel present, connected to those beside me.

I want to feel creative, stimulated by energies shared.

I want to feel love, the authentic warmth of being cared.

I want to feel bonded by likeminded friends.

I want to feel adventure that seemingly never ends.

I want to feel full of laughter and fond memories.

I want to feel this way, every day, and do so with ease.

The Gold Can Stay

The words of Mr. Frost caught my eye today.

His poem title says it all,

"Nothing Gold Can Stay"

He described flowers blooming

as the bud becomes a leaf.

Then he mentions how they die,

"So, Eden sank to grief."

His concept is clear,

and thoughts well written.

But there is something I must say:

The idea of gold is one's to behold.

So, I say, the gold can stay.

Who is to claim the falling leaf

isn't as beautiful as the bloom?

All elements possess beauty,

even down to the tomb.

The Present

I enjoy the times of absolute presence,

the gift of being fully aware,

able to capture an entire essence

in all the senses of life's wonderful elements.

Though a moment only lasts

but a brief instant,

it can give off a sensation that lingers

longer than the breath it was captured in.

That is the beauty of the "present"

for it can also be regifted,

used for when the "now" is bleak,

wrapped in the magnificent sheen

of one's own memory.

Then replayed again and again

for the sake of feeling the warmth

when the current climate is cold.

Bonded by Division

Two mindsets
that work entirely
on different waves.
For their motives
and deepest desires
lie on opposite ends.
Constantly at war
with the concept
of what to truly value.
For the reign of happiness
is often shadowed by pain.
With the clarity to see,
I know there is still fog
in my vision.
Altering between egos
of myself and I.
Bonded by division,
fighting heart against mind.

Quarter Century

I have woken to the sunrise, fallen asleep under moonshine,

spent days dancing in the sun, and
nights cradled by good wine.

I have had laughs that hurt, cries that soothed,

lovers that had failed, cherished ones who have moved.

I have been shattered by the closest, rebuilt by the unexpected.

I still hesitate to love, but eager to feel my heart protected.

I have gained a successful foundation, with a roof over my head,

thankful for those authentic few, for their love never misled.

I feel blessed for my time, and pray the end is not near,

and now I will celebrate, for my quarter century is here!

Nightmare of Complacency

Before fully waking from a night of restlessness,
I grabbed the journal from the side of my bed.
With half asleep visions,
I began to write what my mind could not yet grasp.
My dream spiraled out of me:
I entered the shallow waters,
succumbing to its effortless manner.
There was no current,
no wave to worry,
just a glossy surface.
My body slowly submerged
in the lukewarm, still sea.
My movement failed to create even the slightest ripple.
As I stared into my reflection,
a glaze fell over my eyes.
I lay down
with a numbing mediocrity.
And I allow it to take me away,
floating, floating, floating.

I Reject the Script

I reject the script
that seems to flow
within those people
too afraid to grow,
or think outside the box.
Stories are told
with intent to provoke
the emotions of "their" choosing.
And designed to keep
all who listen
under their full control.
I reject the script,
the rehearsed plot
showcased in various ways,
trained to keep all
trapped in its cycle,
taught by those
who devour
spoon-fed comfort.
For they themselves

dislike the taste
of curiosity.
I reject the script
of societal norms.
To find my own way
with eyes open to explore
and questions to ask.
I shall be designed
entirely by the construct
of my own mind.
For my vision of life
is the way in which
I will thrive.
I reject the script.

Sit

It was an early rise this October morning,

the air still warm from faded summer.

I arrive to the beach, coffee in hand

and I begin to casually wander.

My toes in the sand with the wind in my hair,

this is where I am now.

Weeks of speed caught up to me.

A wave of exhaustion held me down.

Petting the dog that is passing by,

I cannot help but smile wide.

Then I sit beside a surfer,

having conversation on the morning tide.

To be with the wondrous ocean,

this is the moment I know I need.

I watch its sensual grace

and admire the waves' delicate speed.

It is rare to capture these instants,

when living life at a fast pace.

So today I wish to sit and breathe,

to only feel the sunshine upon my face.

Mourn

Many chapters of my life have been written.

Time has been spent with people no longer in my days.

With the vision always on tomorrow,

I admit I never mourned the years that passed

or the relationships that fell to the wayside,

until I see the familiar old face,

or stand in a place I once frequented.

It is then, a wave of sorrow fills my heart

as I say goodbye to the friend,

or take a final glance back,

I wish I could remember

all the infinite details

that once were the stories of my days.

The smells, the feels,

all the excitement.

The ecstasy within the simplicity

of where I used to be.

Gift or Curse?

Is it a gift or a curse?
To have the visibility to see
that all of life is what you make it.
No longer blinded by collective ideas.
I get to decide all of who I am
from my values to my perception,
all of it is mine to hold.
But that concept is daunting,
for the ease and comfort to obey
is no longer an option I can entertain.
So now what?
As I sit in solitude,
battling every notion fathomable,
I keep returning to one question.
Is it a gift or a curse?
To have the visibility to see
that all of life is what you make it.

Love

What I Am After

Bring me devotion with excitement, so together we may shine.

I am not after the world, just the quality of your time.

Let us dive deep without boundaries, show off your colors.

Keep your heart safe with me, do not fool with others.

Lie lazy in my arms or run wild with my soul.

Be your own person, but together we become whole.

Fall in love with our moments and smile at me wide.

Be with me entirely and set your worries aside.

Right Before He Kissed Me

After our wit-filled conversation subsided, he and I sat together for a while. We let silence consume the empty space. Within a few more moments we inch a little closer, gradually falling into one another. Our bodies start the communication we were trying to hide. Or, at least, that I was trying to hide.

Slowly placing my head down on his chest, I hear his beating heart. It plays a soothing rhythm that sends my worries away. Cooing at the feel of his breath over my cheek, I then snuggle deeper into him. I love the little nook under his chin. His scent gives me a high I cannot match, and I simply melt while lying in his arms. I am so drawn to him. It is a feeling I cannot control.

I look up as we hold one another, and playfully rub my nose to his. An elated smile spreads on his face. My eyes capture his warming authenticity, and it sets my heart aflame. He places his lips onto mine. My mind freezes momentarily, but the feel of his lips on mine was all I desired. I stare at him closely, his hand still under my chin. Then I kiss him again, deeply, knowing very well the consequences to follow.

That moment lingered on my mind for days after. Along with questions of our seemingly permanent purgatory. Just like I knew it would. Now in my silence, I go back to that place. That small instant, it replays in my mind. When I close my eyes all I can see is the smile on his face, right before he kissed me.

The Alarm

Somewhere between five and six a.m.

he snuck quietly from my bed.

The room barely aglow from a summer's daybreak,

I heard him fumbling with the tools in the kitchen drawer

then tinker with the alarm in the hall.

What a convenient time for it to set off.

I sighed deeply knowing it woke him.

And felt enraged that it stole his warm body away from mine.

He came back into the room to collect his belongings.

My heart sank from the sound of his car keys in his hand.

Then before he could go I grabbed him tight,

always in fear that it would be our last encounter.

I took down the alarm after he left,

placing it on the ledge in the hall.

Now I walk past it every day.

But in a world where everything I own has "its place"

I leave the alarm untouched.

And I cannot find a reason why.

Fan from Japan

Looking through my belongings today,

I stumbled across a keepsake.

As I picked it up

I smiled upon its loveliness.

Just like I did the first time I saw it.

When I opened it,

I recall the way my heart was beating,

It throbbed from the pure excitement,

For it reminded me of something sweet.

Even from across the world,

with all his mind had to bear,

I was a small thought.

In the form of a beautiful fan from Japan

Blue Glitter

He and I had spent some time a few Christmas seasons ago.

We drove to the store in search of de-
cor, the ground had a dusting of snow.

I ran down the isles to grab frill, the
theme in my mind was blue.

He smiled and laughed at the regis-
ter, as I threw in a Kit Kat or two.

On the way back I made him detour, as
I showed him my family home.

I said, "go here." We turned the truck and began to roam.

I brought him down a familiar street, where
I knew the lights were a show.

Confused, he asked, "Why did I listen?" I
said, "Just a little farther to go."

We came to the corner and there it was,
a block of spectacular cheer.

"I told you it would be worth it," I said, a cheeky sneer.

That evening we hung up the lights.
Blue glitter covered the floor.

He watched me decorate as I asked him
to hand me a piece more.

After it was done, we sat on the couch. My
work and my vision he did approve.

We then lay together in the aura of blue, let-
ting the ambiance take over our mood.

I Have a Scar

I have a scar,

a little less than an inch long.

It sits center, under my diaphragm.

You saw it,

on one of our nights together.

You gave a line.

"The scars you see aren't the wounds
she's afraid of getting again".

I rub my pointer finger over the scar,

the way you did when you saw it.

That moment

leaves me to question,

what else do you see?

What If

I suppress it mostly,
the curiosity of possibilities.
Though frequency was scarce,
our time spent was significant.
Scattered throughout months,
which drew on into years.
Constantly growing with anticipation,
always wanting to know more.
That is what enticed me the most.
You were my favorite story
that I never got to finish.
A cliffhanger that
still leaves me wondering:
What if. . .

Ah but a Kiss

Ah but a kiss, so much within a kiss.

To tell a soul's story can be through a kiss.

To surrender sincerity can be through a kiss.

To magnify devotion can be through a kiss.

To set forth false pretenses can be through a kiss.

To manipulate and control can be through a kiss.

To disassemble one's heart can be through a kiss.

Ah but a kiss, so much within a kiss. . .

Crave

Though it is clear
what never was
will never be,
I find myself unable to resist the want.
An imagination gone too far
for far too long.
A curiosity still unsettled,
even with proof
of its unprogressive state.
I do not know the answer I seek,
for I no longer know the question.
Perplexed by my instinct,
for normally it leads me well.
Is there something I lack?
Or is it just something I lust?
What do I see in him?
Throughout the years
of our undeciphered objective,
there was always something I crave,
Time spent with him.

I Want to Erase Them

I want to erase them,

all the notes involving you.

Because before they were notes,

they only existed in my mind.

The intangibility made it tolerable.

But when I wrote them down

they became real.

Forcing me to see

that you are something unattainable.

With that truth

all I feel

is disappointment.

I fear I have failed.

Pretend

Am I supposed to pretend
that all is just fine?
I spend every minute of the day
preoccupying my time.
To distract me from the truth,
that I am missing him.
I thought I could contain this,
but my heart aches from within.

Dopamine Fiend

Take the quick hit,

enjoy the ride.

Come down crashing,

fight to survive.

All that I am,

ride in these waves.

Unconsciously burrowing,

plotting my days.

Cannot Fall for Potential

You can see it

so clearly.

A vision of everything

that you thought

this person could be.

You wanted it

so badly.

You stayed engaged

longer than you should have.

But even so,

they were never yours.

You still think of them

every now and then.

Though you know

they are wasted thoughts.

Years pass by,

and you wonder,

If the fog consumes them still.

You see them at times

but there is no longer

any real recognition

of who you thought they were.

Because

you fell in love

with their potential

that they never achieved.

"Perfect"

You set this precedent
with the intention
of it being unattainable.
Just so you do not have to
keep anyone close.
You keep preaching
these canned reasons
to stay alone.
To showcase a "strength"
that hinders your ability
to be strong.
So go and hide
behind the mask of a smile.
While your weakness
bleeds through.

Black Widow

Ruins of the old begin to dissipate.

Intrapersonal betrayal ordains new command.

Thirst for domination activates the switch.

Power and control are now the demand.

An entanglement of bodies

that disconnect while connecting.

Foreclosed on intimacy,

rushed by lust.

Satisfaction is now the only gain.

I Must Accept

I must accept

that we never were,

nor will we ever be.

I must accept

that the memories of you

might always sting.

I must accept

that I no longer know you

in the ways I once did.

I must accept

the choices you made

that led to the lives we live now.

I must accept

this is the reality

and my imagination is just that.

I must accept.

I Chose Me

A Haiku

The best choice I made
was when I chose to love me
when you chose not to.

I Let it Go

I kept fear and distrust all around me

disguised in different ways.

Some days it took the form of strength.

Others, it left my mind in a maze.

These feelings were my true comfort.

Convinced they were a friend.

They were but a parasite,

or a wound I refused to mend.

Then I found something remarkable.

A purity behind new eyes.

It was there I felt willing to trust.

His love held an unfamiliar surprise.

With each passing day I learned a little.

Then I discovered something bold to show.

The depth of his heart helped me love.

It was then I let the fear and distrust go.

Memories to Montauk

My thoughts spread wide as the road begins to narrow.

I set the music to tunes that soften my mood.

In anticipation for inspiration, I glide through faces and time.

Trying to decipher my intent, I set-
tle on a pleasant remembrance.

In a time of sunshine and wine, beside my lover.

I reminisce his lips, slightly stained from Cab Franc.

I can feel his exhale on my brow,

and see the pattern of leaves from the maple tree we lie under.

We listened to the poetic birds

whilst feeling the kiss of the cool breeze on our cheeks.

I took this moment, saw it, felt it wholly,

relived each element and savored it slowly.

This wonderful memory came with me

all the way to Montauk.

Tomorrow

I pick up my love tomorrow

after months of being gone.

I have been waiting for this moment

for so very long.

Anticipation through my veins,

like a surging, electric power.

Oh, how I have counted endless days,

every minute, every hour.

I cannot wait to hold him close

in my loving arms once more.

All I see and feel is him now.

It is him who I adore.

Family/ Friends

My Dearest Unknown Children

My dearest unknown children,

how I love you so.

My heart will always be with you,

though inside of me you did not grow.

My dearest unknown children,

I am giving you all that I can,

I pray you enter this world,

to live long and happy as planned.

My dearest unknown children,

I do hope to one day meet.

Although I am anonymous,

it would be a welcomed greet.

My dearest unknown children,

I hope your journey is a success.

With the gift of life, I hope you find,

the desire to be your very best.

Audience of "Friends"

On the stage with the spotlight bright,

with an audience of one-way mirrors.

Keep smiling, keep dancing,

strutting about like a show pony.

Allowing no patron to question

whether or not you are a phony.

Diminish the slightest sign

of sweat dripping from your temple.

And remember to always keep

any real secrets

behind the drawn curtain.

Isolated

I feel isolated
in a room full of people.
I hear, I see, I interact.
But I am not there.
I am locked in my mind,
conversing rehearsed dialogue.
Nodding with a played smile,
just to stay relevant
within a social circle,
with its sole purpose
to make me feel connected.

Fine

Time has passed as it always does,

but my questions still left unchanged.

I often wonder how you are,

if happiness is something you have obtained.

Last we spoke your vision was blurred

From the falsities of your self-doubt.

I wanted to be the one to help guide you,

the discovery of the real you I hoped to hear about.

Our worlds look a little different now,

and I know I ought to stay the line.

But how I wish to talk to you more,

to know that you are more than just "fine".

Reality?

Haze engulfs the trees in the distance, its ac-
complice is a thicket of grey.

The elusive blanket trances the mind,
forming a sense of disarray.

Tangibility of the known, now unveils an eerie uncertainty.

Lost in the thought of what holds truth,
wandering in a fogged reality.

Unloved

A Haiku

Family is love?

Then why do I feel unloved?

Judged and unwelcomed.

Leave Me Be with the Memory of You

I find comfort in your absence now.

It is the emptiness that I hold true.

The vacancy my body feels is real.

It is the only real part left

of you and me.

My hero you were,

struck down by the monstrosities

that you let live

within your own mind.

You have become a hollow shell

of the man I once called "Father."

I wish you would just go

like you intended to.

And leave me be

to mourn the loss

of the memory of you.

Imagine

Imagine
staring into the eyes
of the eyes
who created you.
Wishing nothing more
than their departure
from this world.
Knowing that
a part of you
will die with them.
But feeling that
this death
is the only way
to be free.
To live life
unburdened
from constant disarray.
Imagine. . .

Numbness

I feel numbness in my soul
from continuously
forcing my emotions
to stay silent.
I thought it would be easier
to go on without them.
Though maybe it is,
life now seems uninteresting.
I am unable to find
the sensations
in anything around me.
It is as if
my days lived
are only seen
in black and white.
No longer felt
in the vibrant colors
they were once created in.
I take the blame
for dulling the energy

within myself.
Now I am left
with this feeling
of nothing.

Force

I have forced myself to ignore
the most authentic needs.
In efforts to alleviate the pain
that is associated with
being unable to obtain them.
But then when those needs are given,
I become deeply distressed.
Because it is too late,
and I am already too far gone.
Jaded from the anguish
of not receiving those needs
when it mattered the most.

Rehtorb

Backwards, the relationship you and I share.

Months and years continue to pass

as time distances us without a care.

Though our blood is the same

we know less of each other than water.

Condemned by the same hardships,

yet we share no bond with one another.

They say that history repeats itself,

I can understand that tale.

Our family ties are cursed with strife,

with no vision on how to prevail.

But maybe if we try, we can do better.

You and I have nothing to lose,

except the chance of a relationship forever.

I long to live past your guarded walls,

wishing to undo the damage done to us.

Perhaps one day we could start anew

and share something more than fear and mistrust.

Hello Mother

Hello Mother,

it is good to see you.

It is rare that I do.

Most days you are gone.

Vices keep you withdrawn.

Then they hold onto you for so long.

Hello Mother,

it is good to see you.

It is rare that I do.

I see the pain you go through.

How your happy days seem so few.

Haunted by a past you wish you could undo.

Hello Mother,

it is good to see you.

It is rare that I do.

But when you are here,

you are wonderful and clear,

smiling, cooking, and sincere.

Hello Mother,

it is good to see you.

It is rare that I do.

But I need you to know,

no matter the darkness you show,

I will always love you so.

Chess

I brought out the board and then came the smile,

drawn widely across his face.

We sat down to talk less for a while,

I have uncovered a new happy place.

He let me start as I set Queen's Gambit,

trying to stay one step ahead.

In this arena he made all the right moves

while I fought and struggled to tread.

I picked up strategy as the game settled in.

He laughed as I made a move he did not see.

In that moment he could tell I was his kin,

he let me know how proud he was of me.

A few moves later I pushed to attack,

taking his favorite piece, the knight.

With a nervous grin he saw his slack,

he knew he had to put up a stronger fight.

We played for hours in a friendly flow,

a dynamic I never thought could be.

In the game of chess, he and I can grow.

Forever grateful, the winner will always be we.

Your Flow of Thought

Your Flow of Thought

Your Flow of Thought

Your Flow of Thought

_____

_____

_____

_____

_____

_____

_____

_____

_____

_____

_____

_____

_____

_____

_____

_____

_____

_____

_____

_____

_____

_____

Your Flow of Thought

Your Flow of Thought

Your Flow of Thought

Your Flow of Thought

Your Flow of Thought

Made in the USA
Coppell, TX
11 February 2022

73413688R00046